My Little
BOOK OF
BIBLE STORIES

CANDLE
BOOKS

INTRODUCTION

Children will love to listen to this collection of eight Bible stories. But even more, they will be encouraged to join in the fun by pointing, repeating, making sounds, and answering questions. Best of all, these books present Bible stories and truths in simple words a young child can understand. Little ones can learn so much about God!

CONTENTS

Published in the USA in 2003 by Candle Books
(a publishing imprint of Lion Hudson plc).
Reprinted 2004

ISBN 0 8254 7278 4

Distributed by Kregel Publications, PO Box 2607,
Grand Rapids, Michigan 49501.

Coedition arranged by Lion Hudson plc,
Mayfield House, 256 Banbury Road, Oxford OX2 7DH
Tel: +44 (0) 1865 302750   Fax: +44 (0) 1865 302757
Email: coed@lionhudson.com
www.lionhudson.com

Printed in Singapore.

My Little
BOOK OF BIBLE STORIES

The story of Creation provides wonderful opportunities for your child to learn about God's world. As you read this story, stop after the questions to allow your child to respond by pointing to the pictures.
He will not only learn about God's world, he will also learn the deeper lesson behind the story – the lesson of God's love and power.

This story is taken from Genesis 1 & 2.

SOMEONE TO LOVE

THE STORY OF CREATION

Long, long ago, there was God.
But there were no people
for God to love.

No big people.
No little people.
Not even any
baby people.

And the world was a dark and empty place.

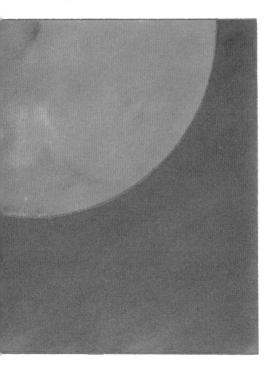

Then God said,
"Let there be light!"

And there was light.

And the light was good.

But there were still no people
for God to love.

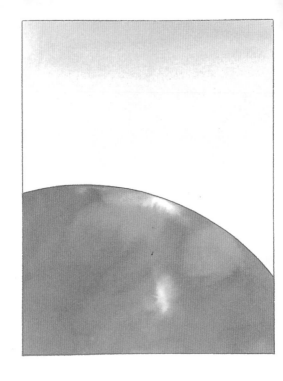

God made day.

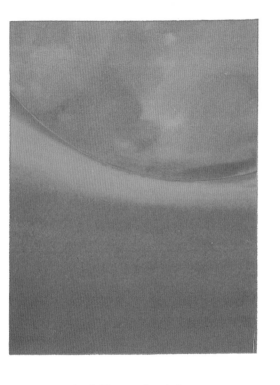

And He made night.

He made the beautiful blue sky.
And it was good.

16

But there were still no people
for God to love.

God moved the waters to one place
so there would be dry ground.

Then God made plants and trees.

Where is the apple tree?

Where is the orange tree?

Where are the strawberry plants?

Where are the banana trees?

God put the big, yellow sun
in the daytime sky.
He put twinkling stars and a glowing moon
in the night sky.

And the plants and trees
and sun and stars were all very good.
But there were still no people
for God to love. 23

Then, God made birds to fly in the sky.
Where is the red bird?
Where is the yellow bird?
Where is the blue bird?

God made fish to swim in the sea.
Do you see the big fish?
Do you see the little fish?

25

God made animals
to run and play in the green grass.

Can you count the animals?

God's world was no longer empty.
It was full of wonderful things.
But there were still no people
for God to love.

So God made a man and a woman.
God named the man Adam.

Adam named the woman Eve.

Now there were people for God to love.

And since that time,
God has loved all the big people,
and all the little people,

and all the baby people
who have ever lived
in His beautiful world.

Noah's Ark has long been a favourite of young children. In addition to learning about Noah's faith and God's faithfulness your child will have fun learning animal sounds and rainbow colours. After each question on pages 46-53, stop and allow your child to tell you what each animal says. Page 63 can be used two ways to teach colours. You may point and ask your child to say the colour, or you may wish to say the colour and ask your child to point to it. Share with your little ones in simple words your own faith in God.

This story is taken from
Genesis 6-8

Two By Two

THE STORY OF NOAH'S FAITH

Noah was God's friend.
He believed what God said ...
God always tells the truth.

One day, God told Noah
there would be a flood.
"You must build
a great big boat," God said.

Nobody knew what a flood was.

But Noah believed God.

So he gathered enough wood
to build a great big boat.
Tap, tap, tap. Rap, rap, rap.

Noah worked very hard.
He made the boat
just the way God told Him to,
for Noah believed everything God said.

People came to see what Noah was doing.
When they saw the big boat,
they laughed and laughed.
"There is no water here!" they said.
"Where will you float your boat?"

Noah told the people what God said,
but they did not believe.
Noah went back to work.
He knew what God said was true.

One day the boat was finished.
"Now," God said,
"I will bring two of every kind of animal

to ride on the boat with you."
Noah waited for the animals to come.

The frisky puppies came two by two.
What do the puppies say to you? (bow, wow)

The soft furry kittens came two by two.
What do the kittens say to you? (meow)

The waddling ducks came two by two.
What do the ducks say to you? (quack, quack)

The spotted cows came two by two.
What do the cows say to you? (moo)

49

The curly-tailed pigs came two by two.
What do the pigs say to you? (oink, oink)

50

The woolly sheep came two by two.
What do the sheep say to you? (baa, baa)

51

The tiny mice came two by two.
What do the mice say to you? *(squeek, squeek)*

The great big bears came two by two.
What do the bears say to you? (grrrrrr)

53

The animals came two by two,
elephants, lions and monkeys, too.
Noah led them all into the boat.

"Bang!" God shut the door.
They were all safe inside.

Drip, drip, drip
the raindrops fell softly.
Splish, splash, splish.
They made puddles on the ground.

56

The lightning flashed!
The thunder cracked!
Down, down, down
the heavy rain fell.

57

Noah's boat rocked
a little this way
and a little that way.
It was starting to float.

58

For forty days and forty nights
it rained, and rained, and rained.
The water rose higher and higher.
And the big boat stayed right on top
with Noah and the animals safe inside.

Then something happened. Noah listened.
He did not hear the rain.

Slowly, very slowly,
the flood waters dried away.

One day, the big boat landed
on the top of a large mountain.

When God said it was time,
Noah let the animals out of the boat.
Two by two they marched
down the mountain
to look for new homes.

I will never again
cover the earth with water," God promised.
"And as a reminder,
I will put a rainbow in the sky."

Can you tell me the colours of the rainbow?
(red, orange, yellow, green, blue, purple)

Noah looked at the beautiful rainbow.
He knew what God promised was true.

And Noah was very glad
he believed God.

The story of Joseph is one that every small child can relate to. So often, little ones are rejected by older brothers, sisters and neighbour children. It will encourage your child to know that, in time, he or she will grow up and have a good relationship with siblings. Meanwhile, help your little one feel bigger by teaching him to "read" the capitalised words in the story. After your child becomes familiar with the story, pause when you come to the words printed in capitals and allow your child to fill them in. "Get Lost, Little Brother" is a fun way for your child to learn about trusting God and forgiving others.

This story is taken from
Genesis 37-45

"Get Lost, Little Brother"

THE STORY OF JOSEPH

Joseph's father gave him a new coat. Oooh, it was beautiful.

None of his brothers
had one like it.
They felt LEFT OUT.

Joseph was HAPPY,
but his brothers were MAD.

They went outside by themselves.
And they left Joseph behind.

"Go find your brothers,"
Joseph's father said one day.
So Joseph went to look for them.

Flip, flop, flippity, flap.
His sandals slapped
against the ground.

Joseph looked and looked.
Finally he found his brothers.

But they were still ANGRY.
They did not want to see
"Little Brother" again.

They took away his beautiful coat
and threw him into a deep, dark hole.

Down, down Joseph tumbled.
Thump, thump, bumpity, bump.
"Help! Help!" he cried.
But they would not listen.

"Let's send him away," his brothers said.
"Then he will be gone for good."

Crunch, crunch, crunchity, crunch.
The camels took Joseph away to Egypt.

Joseph was LONELY.
He wanted to go HOME.
But God had a special job for him.

Joseph grew bigger.
And older.
And stronger.
And wiser.

One day, GOD gave Joseph
a message for the king.

"For seven years there will be lots of food.
Then for seven years there will be none."

"What should we do?" asked the king.
Without food we will all die!"

Joseph answered,
"We must save all the food we can.
Then there will be plenty
when we need it."

The king was HAPPY.
He made Joseph his special helper.

The king gave him a new robe.
Joseph was very important now.
Everyone in Egypt had to obey him.

Joseph told the people
to fill big barns with grain.

After seven years,
everyone ran out of food.
But Joseph had plenty.

89

Hungry people with growling
tummies came to Egypt.
Rumble, grumble, gurgle, grrr.
They wanted something to eat.

Even Joseph's brothers came.
Rumble, grumble, gurgle, grrr.
They were hungry, too!

His brothers did not know who Joseph was.
He looked different now.
But Joseph knew them.

"I am Joseph!," he cried.
They were AFRAID,
but Joseph hugged and kissed them all.

"Now I know why God
brought me to Egypt," he said.
"God brought me here
to save my family."

And that made Joseph
HAPPIER THAN HE HAD
EVER BEEN BEFORE.

The story of Moses crossing the Red Sea has a continuing fascination for children and adults. "Who Needs A Boat?" will bring the story to life for your little ones and give them a vivid reminder of God's power and protection. After you have read the story to your child several times, allow him or her to fill in the italicised words. The poem on the last page is a paraphrase of the song Moses sang. Your little one can memorise it easily and will delight in saying it with you as you read it.

This story is taken from
Exodus 3-15

WHO NEEDS A BOAT?

THE STORY OF MOSES

For Moses, it seemed like
it was going to be
just an ordinary day.

But suddenly a bush caught fire!

And God spoke to Moses.

"I have heard my people crying," God said, "and I am sending *you* to lead them out of Egypt."

So Moses went to see the king.

"God says to let His people go!"
Moses told him.

But the king replied,
"I do not know God,
and I will *NOT*
let the people go!"

So God sent
frogs to … *jump in the king's bed*
and flies to … *buzz in his ears*
and gnats to … *crawl on his nose*
and grasshoppers to … *eat his plants*
and a lot of other things
to make the king … *change his mind.*

And it worked.

"Go!" shouted the king.
"Take the people! Take the sheep!
Just take them all and *GO!*"

So the people followed Moses
out of Egypt. They walked and walked
'til they came to the sea.

108

There was no bridge.
They had no boats.
How would they get across?

Then the people heard
a noise like thunder,
but it was not a rainstorm.

It was worse than that!

It was the king's army
thundering toward the sea!

The soldiers were coming
to take God's people back to Egypt.

The people cried out in fear.

Moses tried to calm them.
"Do not *be afraid*," he said,
"God will fight for you."

Then God told Moses
to hold his rod
out over the water.

And Moses did.

And the sea opened
right down the middle.

It opened wider and wider.

Walls of water rose higher and higher.

Moses and the people walked
through the sea
on the road God made for them.

What a funny sight it was!

When they were safe on the other side,
the people turned around to watch.

The army was still coming!

Moses lifted his rod,
and *God* brought all the water
splashing down.

The king's army was swished away
never to bother
God's people again.

Moses and the people
were thankful for God's help,
so they sang this happy song:

"The Lord is my strength,
The Lord is my song,
I'll praise my God,
All the day long."

Preschool children sometimes feel very small. Older brothers and sisters and other children are able to do so many things. Through the story of David, your little one will learn that doing little jobs well will lead to bigger things. Involve your child in the story each time by allowing him to count the sheep on pages 134 and 135. Once your little one knows the story, pause when you come to a highlighted word and wait for your child to fill in the word.

This story is taken from
1 Samuel 16 and 17

"I MAY BE LITTLE"

THE STORY OF DAVID'S GROWTH

Long ago in a land far away lived a little boy named David.

He had seven brothers
who were older …
and bigger …
and stronger
than David.

They did not want
a little boy in the way
while they were working.

Sometimes David felt
very small and unimportant.

But one day his father gave him
a job of his very own.
He asked David to be a shepherd.

A shepherd is someone
who watches the sheep.

A shepherd counts his sheep
to make sure they are all with him.

133

You can learn to count the sheep too!

135

A shepherd leads his sheep
to food and water.
He puts medicine on their scratches.

A shepherd loves his sheep.

David was glad
to have a job to do.

"I may be little
but God will help me
do big things!"

David took his sheep to the grassy hills.
He watched while the big sheep ate lunch

He laughed when the little lambs romped
and rolled among the wildflowers.

141

But sometimes David felt lonely.
There was nobody to play with.

So David made up songs
to remind himself
that God was always near.

143

David spent many hours
talking to God.

They became best friends.

David knew God could help him
become a good shepherd.
God could help him
protect his sheep from hungry animals.

Often, David practiced throwing rocks
with his sling ...
and he learned to hit his target
every time.

Once a growling bear came
and chased the little lambs.
Round and round David whirled his sling . .
then *zing-g-g* went a stone through the air.

Whack-k-k went the stone
on the big bear's snout.
Gr-r-r-r went the bear as he zipped away
through the bramble bushes.

149

Another day a ferocious lion
spied David's sheep.
He wanted lamburgers for lunch!

With one big bound
the lion pounced on a fluffy lamb
and snatched it away from its mother. 151

There was no time to use his sling.
David ran as fast as he could.
He knew God would help him
save his sheep.

Before the lion knew what happened,
David grabbed him by the mane
and bopped him on the head.

153

The fluffy lamb was safe ...
and David was happy.
He had done a good job.

"I may be little,
but with God's help
I can do big things!"

The story of Jonah is filled with action. Your child will giggle as you stress the highlighted onomatopoeia (sound suggests meaning) words in the first few readings. Soon, your little one will be able to say the words with you. When you feel your child knows these special words, pause when you come to them and allow him or her to fill in the word. Remember, your child's laughter does not mean he is not taking the lesson to heart. It only means you will be asked to read the story again and again. As God's truth is presented repeatedly, your child's understanding will grow.

This story is taken from the Book of Jonah

"I Don't Want To"

THE STORY OF JONAH

God spoke to Jonah.
What did He say?
"Go! Go to preach in Nineveh."

NINEVEH →

But Jonah was not happy.
"I don't want to!,"
Jonah said to himself,
"and I won't go."

"I will pack my things and run away.
I will go so far
God will never find me."

Jonah hurried to the shore.

He paid for a ride on a big boat.

"God will not find me here," Jonah thought

But God sees wherever we are.
He hears whatever we think.
God knew where Jonah was.

167

And God sent a storm to tell him so.

The wind went *whish*!
The waves went *swish*!
And the big boat was tossed to and fro.

Zing went Jonah right out of the boat.
Splash went Jonah right into the sea.

Glub ... glub ... glub went Jonah
as he sank slowly to the bottom.

But God did not want Jonah to drown.

So God sent a great *BIG* fish ...

... to swallow Jonah!

Slippery, *slimy*.
Jonah slid to the fish's belly.
Ishy, *squishy*.
What a place to be!

It was dark inside the fish.
It was hot inside the fish.
It was stinky inside the fish.
Phewy!

Whoosh, *swoosh* went the fish's stomach
Thump, *thump* went Jonah's heart.
It was time to pray!
Now, Jonah wanted to obey.

God heard Jonah's prayer.

He sent the fish to shore.

Zing went Jonah right out of the fish.
Splat went Jonah right onto the beach.

"Moan, moan, groan," went Jonah as he picked himself up from the ground.

God spoke to Jonah.
What did He say?
"Go! Go to preach in Nineveh!"

And what do you think
Jonah did this time?

He headed for Nineveh in a hurry!

Jonah had learned to quickly obey.

NINEVEH →

185

NO TREE FOR CHRISTMAS will offer your child the opportunity to feel the excitement of the shepherds as they searched for and found God's Son. The story of Jesus' birth is told from a different perspective emphasising the fact that Jesus is God and that He is what Christmas is really all about.

Your little one will enjoy answering the questions throughout the book after the story has been told a time or two. Be sure to pause after questions to allow your child to fill in the answers.

At the end of the story, why not take a moment to worship with your child with a one-sentence prayer or by singing "Away in a Manger".

This story is taken from Luke 2

No Tree For Christmas

THE STORY OF JESUS' BIRTH

Was it a naughty lamb sneaking away?

No.

Was it a thief stealing wool for a coat?

No.

191

Was it a wild animal looking for supper?

No.

What could it be?

It was an angel!

The shepherds were so frightened
their knees were quaking

and their hands were shaking.
And they weren't faking!
They had never seen an angel before.

"Do not be afraid," said the angel.
"I have good news for you.
... happy news for all the world!"

"A Savior was born today.
He is the Lord!
"You will find Him in Bethlehem
sleeping in a manger."

When the angel went back to Heaven,
The shepherds went to look
for God's special baby.

This was the most exciting thing
they had ever done!

When they came to Bethlehem,
they searched the stables one by one.
Was this the place they were looking for?
No.

Was this the place they were looking for?
No.

Was THIS the place they were looking for?
No.

But they kept searching.
Do you think they found the right stable?

Yes!

This was it!

Here was the baby in a manger
just like the angel said.

The shepherds came closer
to look at this very special baby.

They were filled with wonder.
Why?

Because Baby Jesus was the Son of God.

He came to bring love and forgiveness to people everywhere.

This was the very first Christmas,
and it was the best of all.

The shepherds did not need lighted trees
or brightly-wrapped presents
or candy-filled stockings to be happy.

They were happy just to see God's Son,
so they got down on their knees
to worship Him.

hey thanked Him, and praised Him,
nd said to Him, "We love You, Lord Jesus!"

215

The book "NOW I SEE" tells the story of a blind man who receives his sight and much more. Young children often respond to handicaps with curiosity and compassion. To help your little one understand blindness, turn off the lights at night for a minute as you talk about the man who never saw anything but darkness. As you read the story, pause at the designated words and allow your child to say the word and/or point to the picture. This story will help your child learn about God's love and His desire to heal our hurts. Your little one will also learn that it is not enough just to know about Jesus. We must respond to Him with faith and obedience.

This story is taken from John 9

"Now I See"

THE STORY OF THE MAN BORN BLIND

Once there was a man
who had been blind
since he was born.
He had never seen anything
but darkness.

He loved the smell of warm *bread*,
but he did not know what bread looked like.

He could feel the silky fur of a *puppy*,
but he could not see a puppy.

He could hear the sweet song
of a *bird* outside his window,
but he had never seen a little bird.

Not even once.

One day, Jesus walked by.
He felt sorry for the blind man,
so He stopped to help.

Smoosh! The man felt cold, wet
mud on his eyes.
And then he heard the kindest voice
he had ever heard …
"Go to the pool and wash."

The man did not argue.
He just obeyed.

He went to the pool and washed his face.

Blink! Blink! Blink!
He opened his eyes wide.
He could see!

At last he could see blue *water*
and yellow and orange *fish*
and white *ducks* and red *flowers*

and green *frogs*
and purple *butterflies*
and anything else there was to see.

231

When the man came home seeing,
his neighbours wanted to know
how it happened.

The man told them that
Jesus had healed him.

But the people did not believe him.
They said terrible things about Jesus.

Then they sent the man away.

Jesus heard what the people
had said to the man.

So Jesus came to find him.

"Do you believe in
the Son of God?" Jesus asked.
The man wanted to know more.

"Tell me who He is so I can believe!"

"You are looking at Him," Jesus answered.
And the man said,
"Lord, I believe! I believe in You!"

"Listen," said the man to his neighbours,
"I have something to say:

Jesus, God's Son, healed me *twice* today!"

"My eyes were blind,
but now I *see*.

My heart was blind,
but now I *believe*."